HOT TOPICS

Hands-on activities ● Investigations ● Model-making … and much more!

Pirates

ages
5–11
for all primary years

Peter Riley

Author
Peter Riley

Editor
Roanne Charles

Assistant Editor
Niamh O'Carroll

Cover and inside illustrations
Laszlo Veres/Beehive Illustration

Photocopiable page illustrations
Colin Elgie

Back cover and inside photography
Peter Rowe

Model-making
Linda Jones

Polaroid photos
Linda Jones. Except pages 19 (bottom), 36 and 66, Peter Rowe.

Series Designer
Helen Taylor

Designers
Helen Taylor and Andrea Lewis

Cover concept/designer
Helen Taylor

Text © 2007 Peter Riley

© 2007 Scholastic Ltd

Designed using Adobe InDesign

Published by Scholastic Ltd
Book End
Range Road
Witney
Oxfordshire OX29 0YD

www.scholastic.co.uk

Printed in the UK by
Bell & Bain Ltd, Glasgow

3 4 5 6 7 8 9   0 1 2 3 4 5 6

British Library Cataloguing-in-Publication Data
A catalogue record for this book is available from the British Library.

ISBN 978-0439-94552-3

The rights of the author Peter Riley have been asserted in accordance with the Copyright, Designs and Patents Act 1988.

Crown copyright material is reproduced under the terms of the Click Use Licence.

The publishers gratefully acknowledge:
Early Learning Centre for the use of pirate ship, rowing boat, pirates and accessories for photography www.elc.co.uk

Due to the nature of the web, the publisher cannot guarantee the content or links of any of the websites referred to. It is the responsibility of the reader to assess the suitability of websites.

Every effort has been made to trace copyright holders for the works reproduced in this book, and the publishers apologise for any inadvertent omissions.

Mixed Sources
Product group from well-managed forests and other controlled sources
www.fsc.org Cert no. TT-COC-002769
© 1996 Forest Stewardship Council
FSC

Contents

PHOTOGRAPH © PETER ROWE. MODEL PIRATES © EARLY LEARNING CENTRE

HOT TOPICS Pirates

Introduction

The *Hot Topics* series explores topics that can be taught across the curriculum. Each book divides its topic into a number of themes that can be worked through progressively to build up a firm foundation of knowledge and provide opportunities for developing a wide range of skills. Each theme provides background information and three lesson plans, for ages 5–7, 7–9 and 9–11. Each lesson plan looks at a different aspect of the theme and varies in complexity from a simple approach with younger children to a more complex approach with older children. There are also photocopiable pages to support the lessons in each theme.

Background information

Each theme starts by providing information to support you in teaching the lesson. You may share it with the children as part of your own lesson plan or use it to help answer some the children's questions as they arise. Information is given about the photocopiable sheets as well as the answers to any questions which have been set. This section also provides a brief overview of all three lessons to help you select content for your own sessions.

The lessons

A detailed structure is provided for lessons aimed at children who are in the 7–9 age range. Less detailed plans, covering all the essentials, are given for the lessons aimed at the other two age ranges so covering the entire primary age range.

Detailed lesson plans

The detailed lesson plans have the following format:

Objectives

The content of all lesson plans is focused on specific objectives related to the study of pirates.

Subject references

All lesson plans show how they relate to specific curriculum-related objectives. These objectives are based on statements in the National Curriculum in England. They may be used as they are, or regarded as an illustration of the statements that may be addressed, helping you to find others which you consider more appropriate for your needs.

Resources and preparation

This section lists everything you will need to deliver the lesson, including any photocopiables provided in this book. Preparation describes anything that needs to be done in advance of the lesson, for example making model ships for Theme 3 Lesson 1 on page 25. As part of the preparation you should consult your school's policies on all practical work so that you can select activities for which you are confident to take responsibility. The ASE publication *Be Safe!* (ISBN 0-863-57324-X) gives useful guidance for conducting safe science activities.

Starter

A Starter is only provided in the more detailed lesson plans for ages 7–9. It provides an introduction to the lesson, helping the children to focus on the topic and generate interest.

What to do

This section sets out, point by point, the sequence of activities in the main part of the lesson. It may include activities for you to do, but concentrates mainly on the children's work.

Differentiation

Differentiation is only provided in the more detailed lesson plans for ages 7–9. Suggestions are given for developing strategies for support and extension activities.

Assessment

This section is only provided in the lesson plans for the 7–9 age range. It suggests ways to assess children, either through the product of their work or through looking at how they performed in an activity.

Plenary

A Plenary is only provided in the lesson plans for the 7–9 age range. It shows how children can review their own work and assess their progress in learning about pirates. It is not related to other lessons, but if you are planning a sequence of lessons you may also like to use it to generate interest in future pirate studies.

Outcomes

These are only provided in the lesson plans for the 7–9 age range. They relate to the general objectives. You may wish to add more specific outcomes related to the context in which you use the lesson.

Extension

This section is found in the lesson plans for 5–7 and 9–11 year olds. It allows you to take the initial content of the lesson further.

Flexibility and extra differentiation

As the lessons in each topic are clustered around a particular theme, you may wish to add parts of one lesson to parts of another. For example in Theme 8, 'The fate of the pirates' you may like to add part of Lesson 2 about a shipwreck to Lesson 1 (which deals with the Navy capturing pirates) for the children to consider two fates that could befall pirates.

In the lesson plans for 7–9 year olds, differentiation is addressed directly with its own section. In lessons for the other age groups, differentiation is addressed by providing ideas for extension work. The themes, however, are arranged so that you may also pick activities from the different age groups to provide differentiation. For example, in a lesson for ages 5–7 you may wish to add activities from the lesson for 7–9 year olds in the same theme.

Planning a project

You may like to use the topic for a class or whole-school project culminating in a Pirate Day. This will need considerable preparation, but the result could be a very memorable event! This section provides some suggestions for activities leading up to the day and for a programme of events.

The suggested activities are featured in or based on the lesson plans shown in the third column. Read through each lesson plan to work out how the activity can fit into the context of your Pirate Day.

Times are given for guidance only. Depending on your circumstances, you might want to lengthen or shorten any activity.

Pirate Day: Ages 5–7
Preparation

● Make sure that you have covered all the preparation needed to carry out the lessons on the Pirate Day. If the children are to perform the pirate song and develop a dance, hoist a pirate flag, unfurl a sail and make a spyglass (telescope) for the production, they need to be prepared well in advance of the day.

● If appropriate, send a letter home asking for parents or carers to help make pirate costumes. If you feel that some children will not be able to bring a costume you should collect some items that they could use. You may have a display of pirate books for parents and carers to look at before Pirate Day to inspire them to make costumes.

● As a feature of the day will be a pirate meal, it is important to mention this in the letter home. Suitable food and drinks are: crackers, butter, cheese, slices of cooked beef, boiled eggs, currants, raisins, pineapple, mango and water and lemon cordial (for grog).

Ages 5–7		Activity	Lesson plan	Pages
MORNING	10 minutes	Procession of costumes	The pirate crew Theme 2 Lessons 1 and 2	17, 21, 22
	40 minutes	Testing sails	Under sail Theme 3 Lesson 1	25, 29
	40 minutes	Pirate flags	Pirate times Theme 5 Lesson 1	41, 45
AFTERNOON	40 minutes	Make a treasure chest	Taking the booty Theme 6 lesson 1	49, 53
	30 minutes	Sharing out the treasure	The treasure Theme 7 Lesson1	57, 61
	30 minutes	Identifying a Navy crew and setting them on a ship made from a box	The fate of the pirates Theme 8 Lesson 1	65, 69
	20 minutes	Final rehearsal and performance of 'Off across the Oggin'	Famous pirates Theme 9 lesson 1	73, 77

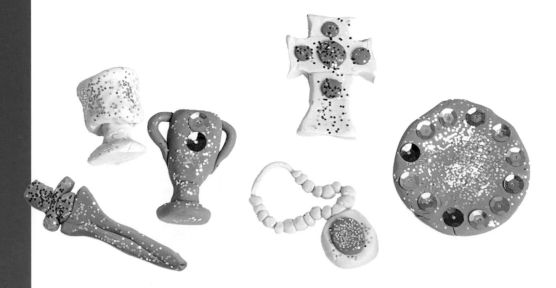

PHOTOGRAPH © PETER ROWE

Pirate Day: ages 7–9
Preparation
- If the children are to perform the pirate song and develop a dance, hoist a pirate flag, unfurl a sail and make a spyglass (telescope) for the production, they need to be prepared well in advance of the day.
- If appropriate, send a letter home asking for parents to help make costumes. If you feel that some children will not be able to bring a costume, collect some items that they could use. You may have a display of pirate books for parents and carers to look at to inspire them to make costumes.
- The day will feature a pirate meal, so mention this in the letter home. Suitable food and drinks are: crackers, butter, cheese, slices of cooked beef, boiled eggs, currants, raisins, pineapple, mango and water and lemon cordial (for grog).
- A day on board ship is divided up into periods of time called 'watches' and each watch is divided up into half-hour units marked by the ringing of a bell (see page 34). You may like to implement the ringing of the bell for the forenoon and afternoon watch as explained there, appointing children to ring the bell at the appropriate time.

Pirate Day: ages 9–11
Preparation
- If the children are to perform the pirate song and develop a dance, hoist a pirate flag, unfurl a sail and make a spyglass (telescope) for the production, they need to be prepared well in advance of the day.
- If appropriate, send a letter home asking for parents to help make costumes. If you feel that some children are unlikely to be able to bring a costume, gather together some items that they could use. You may have a display of pirate books for parents and carers to look at to inspire them.
- A feature of the day will be a pirate meal so mention this in the letter home. See above (Preparation for ages 7–9) for a list of suitable foods.
- The idea behind the day could be that the children are a newly

Ages 7–9		Activity	Lesson plan	Pages
MORNING	40 minutes	Making a sloop and a galleon	Pirate ships Theme 1 Lesson 3	12–15
	30 minutes	The pirate crew	The pirate crew Theme 2 Lesson 2	18–19, 21–2
	40 minutes	Investigating sails and directions	Under sail Theme 3 Lesson 2	26–7, 29–30
	40 minutes	Pirate talk	Life on board Theme 4 Lesson 2	34–5
AFTERNOON	30 minutes	The pirate raid	Taking the booty Theme 6 lesson 2	50–51, 54
	40 minutes	Treasure Island	The treasure Theme 7 Lessons 2 Theme 9 Lesson 2	58–9, 74–5, 78
	40 minutes	Shipwreck	The fate of pirates Theme 9 Lesson 2	66–7
	20 minutes	Final rehearsal and performance of 'Off across the Oggin'	Famous pirates Theme 9 lesson 1	73, 77

Ages 9–11		Activity	Lesson plan	Pages
MORNING	30 minutes	The rules of the crew	The pirate crew Theme 2 lesson 3	20, 22–3
	40 minutes	Talking like a pirate	Under sail Theme 3 Lesson 3	28, 31
	40 minutes	Talking like a pirate	Life on board Theme 4 Lesson 2	34–5
AFTERNOON	30 minutes	Where pirates sailed	Pirate times Theme 5 lesson 2	42–3, 46
	40 minutes	Pirate raid	Taking the booty Theme 6 lesson 2	50–1, 54
	30 minutes	Treasure island	The treasure Theme 7 lesson 2	58–9, 62
	30 minutes	Assessing a pirate life	The fate of pirates Theme 8 lesson 3	68, 71

formed pirate crew preparing to set off on an adventure. In the morning session they consider electing a captain and establishing some rules for life on board ship – just as pirates did. The children could consider how to make the classroom look like a pirate ship and make appropriate decorations. In the afternoon the children discover where pirates sailed, how they made a raid and where they could bury their treasure. Finally, they could assess the pirate way of life and consider whether their popularity today is justified.

Pirate ships

BACKGROUND

Children find pirates exciting. To build on this excitement, this first theme jumps straight into the topic by looking at where pirates spent most of their time – the pirate ship. To set the topic in historical context you may wish to start with Theme 5, 'Pirate times'. The classification of pirate ships is complex and is related to the way the sails were rigged. Square-rigged ships, like the galleon, had sails at right angles to the mast, facing the front of the ship. Ships with fore and aft rigging, like the sloop, had sails facing the side of the ship. Some of the ships which appear in pirate stories are the schooner (two-masted, fore- and aft-rigged), the brig (two-masted, square-rigged), and brigantine (two-masted – front mast square, back mast fore and aft). Pirates used schooners as well as sloops, and they sometimes kept and used larger ships that they captured. These ships, like the galleon, had figureheads that helped to identify them, so pirates would swap the figureheads around to make the ships more difficult to identify.

If you use Theme 4 Lesson 2 (page 34), you might like to introduce a few of the basic terms to describe parts of a ship:
- Bow – the front of the ship.
- Stern – the back of the ship.
- Fore – refers to things at the front of the ship such as the forecastle (fo'c'sle) which is the raised part at the front of a galleon.
- Aft – refers to things at the back of the ship or going in that direction.

- Jib – the front sail on a sloop.
- Bowsprit – the beam protruding from the bow, to which the front sails are attached.
- Main sail – the back sail on a sloop.
- Foremast – the front mast on a galleon.
- Main mast – the second mast.
- Mizzen mast – the third mast.
- Yards – the horizontal beams from which the masts hang.
- Foremast course – the lower sails on the foremast.
- Foremast top sail – the upper sails on the foremast.
- Main course – the lower sail on the main mast.
- Main topsail – the upper sail on the main mast.
- Mizzen course – the sail on the mizzen mast.
- Port – the left side of the ship as you face the bow. This was originally called larboard.
- Starboard – the right side of the ship.

The rigging of the galleon model in this theme is foremast and main mast square and mizzen mast fore and aft. Sails could be set above the top sails; these were called topgallant sails.

THE CONTENTS
Lesson 1 (Ages 5–7)
The sloop
The children make a model of a sloop and learn some names of ship parts.

Lesson 2 (Ages 7–9)
The galleon
The children make a model of a galleon and learn some names of ship parts.

Lesson 3 (Ages 9–11)
The sloop and galleon
The children make models of a sloop and a galleon and learn the names of parts of a ship.

Notes on photocopiables
Make a sloop (page 13)
The main parts of a sloop are provided for cutting out, along with a picture reference.

Make a galleon 1 (page 14)
The main parts of a galleon hull are provided for cutting out.

Make a galleon 2 (page 15)
The stern, sails and figurehead are provided for cutting out.

PHOTOGRAPH © RODOLFO CLIX, STOCK.XCHNG

HOT TOPICS Pirates

Lesson 1 The sloop

Resources and preparation
Each child or group will need: page 13 enlarged and photocopied onto card, a straw, scissors, glue, bluetack and pencils. If possible, make a galleon using pages 14 and 15 before the lesson. For older children, find pictures of sloops or other ships from the 17th century showing how the planks were arranged along the side.

What to do
● Ask the children what they know about pirates. Be prepared for a wide range of answers, from treasure, maps, fighting, parrots and 'talking in a funny way'. From this, focus the discussion on ships.
● Explain how the pirates' preferred ship was the sloop because it was fast and manoeuvrable. Add that pirates sometimes captured and used galleons too.
● You might like to show older children a picture of a sloop and, when you hand out copies of page 13, let them draw lines on the sloop's sides and back to represent planks of wood.
● Hand out the photocopiables and tell the children to cut out the hull, sides and stern, avoiding cutting off the tabs, and stick them together.
● Ask the children to cut out the deck and fold down the tabs, but tell them not to add

glue yet. They should then lower the deck between the sides and the stern.
● Now let the children cut out the sails and bowsprit in one piece. Fold the tabs at right angles and stick to the straw. Stick the straw into a small ball of Blu-Tack on the base of the hull. They should adjust the bowsprit so that it fits in place on the bow.
● Finally, let the children cut out the Jolly Roger. Let the children draw a skull and crossbones on the other side of the flag if they wish, then stick the flag to the top of the mast.
● Display the ships on a table as a pirate fleet. Produce the galleon you have made and tell them this is the treasure ship that they are after.

Extension
● Introduce or revise the terms hull, bow, stern, bowsprit, jib, mast, main sail, port and starboard.
● Mark out the shape of the sloop's hull in the playground and ask the children to sit in it and point out some of the parts of the ship. They could write the terms on cards and put them in the appropriate place.
● Ask the children to give their ship a name. Say that if a ship has a name it is generally a girl's name.

AGES 5–7

Objectives
● To use materials and equipment safely.
● To assemble a model sloop.
● To learn the names of some parts of a ship.

Subject references
History
● Find out about the past from a range of sources.
(NC: KS1 4a)
Design and technology
● Assemble and join components.
(NC: KS1 2d)
English
● Use adventurous and wide-ranging vocabulary.
(NC: KS1 En3 1a)
● Attempt unfamiliar words.
(NC: KS1 En3 2a)

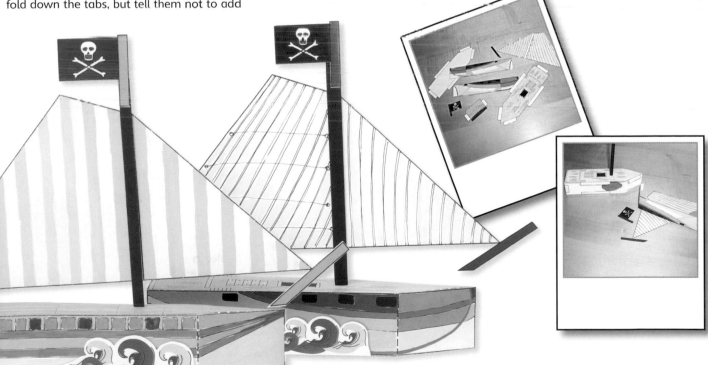

PHOTOGRAPH © PETER ROWE

Lesson 2 The galleon

AGES 7–9

Objectives
● To use materials and equipment safely.
● To assemble a model galleon.
● To learn the names of some parts of a ship.

Subject references
History
● Find out about the past from a range of sources.
(NC: KS2 4a)
Design and technology
● Assemble and join components.
(NC: KS2 2d)
English
●Identify the use and effect of specialist vocabulary
(NC: KS2 En2 5a)
● Attempt unfamiliar words.
(NC: KS1 En3 2a)

Resources and preparation
● Each child or group will need: pages 14 and page 15 enlarged and photocopied onto card, scissors, glue, a straw, Blu-Tack and coloured pencils. Make available pictures of galleons showing how the long planks of wood were arranged along the side of the hull and on the decks.

Starter
● Ask the children what they know already about pirates. Be prepared for a wide range of answers from treasure, maps, fighting, parrots and 'talking in a funny way'. From this, lead the discussion to focus on ships.
● Explain that the most well-known type of ship that pirates sought and attacked was the galleon. Issue the copies of pages 14 and 15.

What to do
● Draw the children's attention to the picture of the finished galleon on page 15 so that they can see how the assembled ship should look.
● Ask the children to draw in the arrangement of planks on the sides and

decks, using the reference pictures of the galleons to help them.
● Start them on cutting out the base, decks and sides on page 14. Note that there are three decks: A – upper deck (poop deck), B – main deck, and C – forecastle deck, which should be separated by cutting lines W to X, and Y to Z.
● Then ask the children to cut out the stern on page 15.
● The children should then bend up the tabs on the base so that they are at right angles to it, apply glue to the tabs on one side and stick a side to it. They should then glue the tabs on the other side and stick a side to it. The tabs on the stern can then be bent at right angles, glue applied to them and the stern can be stuck to the back of the hull.
● The tabs on the decks should then be bent upwards at right angles. Glue should be applied to the tabs of the forecastle deck and the deck should be lowered into position so that the tabs are just below the top of the sides of the hull.
● Glue should be applied to the tabs of the main deck and the deck should be lowered into position so that the tabs are just below the top of the sides of the hull.

PHOTOGRAPH © HERVÉ BOURDON, STOCK.XCHNG

HOTTOPICS Pirates

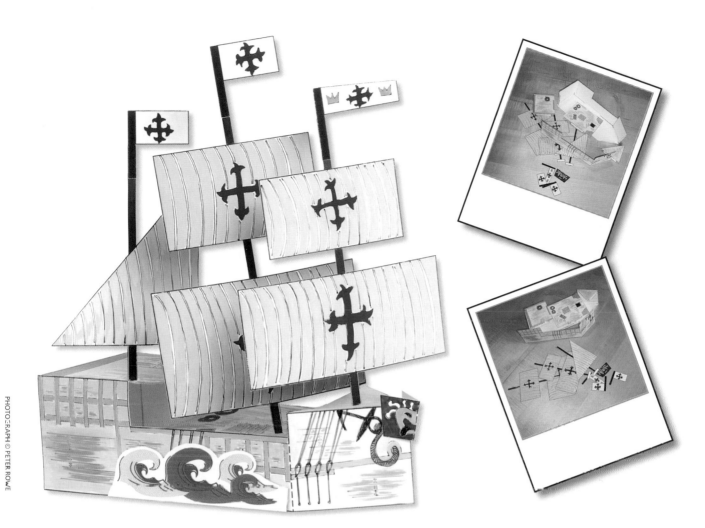

- Similarly, glue should be applied to the tabs of the upper deck and the deck lowered into position so that the tabs are just below the top of the sides of the hull.
- Then ask the children to cut out the three masts on page 15. Each one should be glued to a piece of straw, which is then attached to the hull with a piece of Blu-Tack: the foremast on the foredeck, the main mast on the main deck and the mizzen mast on the upper deck.
- Let the children draw a person or animal on the figurehead mounting before cutting it out, folding it and attaching it to the front of the ship.
- Finally, let the children colour in the flags and banner as they wish but with the aim of making them distinctive and visible from afar. They should mount the banner on the foremast, and the flags on the two other masts. For this activity, it does not matter if the flags appear to be blowing in different directions.

Differentiation

- Some children will need help and supervision when cutting out the template to make sure that the tabs are not cut off. They will also need help in gluing the parts together.
- More confident learners could, when they have made their galleon, also make a pirate sloop to attack it, using a copy of page 13.

Assessment

The children can be assessed on the quality of the construction of their galleon and the visibility of their flags.

Plenary

- Encourage the children to name their ships. Suggest that if it is to be a person's name, ships usually have girls' names.
- Ask the children to arrange their ships on a table and encourage them to talk about them using some of the terms for parts of a ship. Talk about how galleons sailed in convoys as protection against pirates. If some pirate sloops have been made, they can be put in positions where the children think the pirates might be successful if they attacked.

Outcomes

- The children can use materials and equipment safely.
- They can make a model galleon.
- They have acquired vocabulary relating to the parts of a ship.

Lesson 3 The sloop and galleon

AGES 9–11

Objectives
● To learn about two types of ship used in pirate times.
● To assemble two model ships.
● To learn the names of some parts of a ship.

Subject references
History
● Britain and the wider world in Tudor times. (NC: KS2 10)
Design and technology
● Cut and shape a material, join and combine components accurately. (NC: KS2 2d)
English
● Identify the use and effect of specialist vocabulary. (NC: KS2 En2 5a)
Art and design
● Use visual elements including colour and pattern. (NC: KS2 4a)

Resources and preparation
Copy pages 13–15 onto card (see What to do for groupings). The children will need scissors, glue and coloured pencils. This lesson can be adapted as part of your Pirate Day.

What to do
● Share existing knowledge of pirates. Be prepared for the children to suggest a wide range of subjects, including treasure, maps, fighting, parrots and 'talking in a funny way'. From this initial brainstorm, move on to focus on ships.
● Tell the children about the two major types of ship used in pirate times – the sloop, preferred by pirates, and the galleon, used by countries such as Spain to transport valuable goods such as gold and silver.
● Divide the class into two groups, one smaller than the other. Let the children in the smaller group make sloops, and the larger group make galleons. This will result in a more realistic display at the end of the lesson when a small group of pirate sloops can be set up to attack a larger group (a convoy) of galleons.
● Let the children making sloops assemble their ships as in Lesson 1.
● Let those making galleons assemble their ships as in Lesson 2.
● While the children are making their ships, encourage them to use the correct terms for the parts they are cutting out and gluing together.

Extension
When the ships have been made, let the children with the galleons set out their ships in a convoy, deciding how the ships should sail together. Tell them that they can turn one ship into a man-o'-war to protect the rest and let them decide where to place it in the convoy to protect the other ships. Let the children with the sloops decide how to place them around the convoy in order to spring a successful attack.

Theme 1 Make a sloop

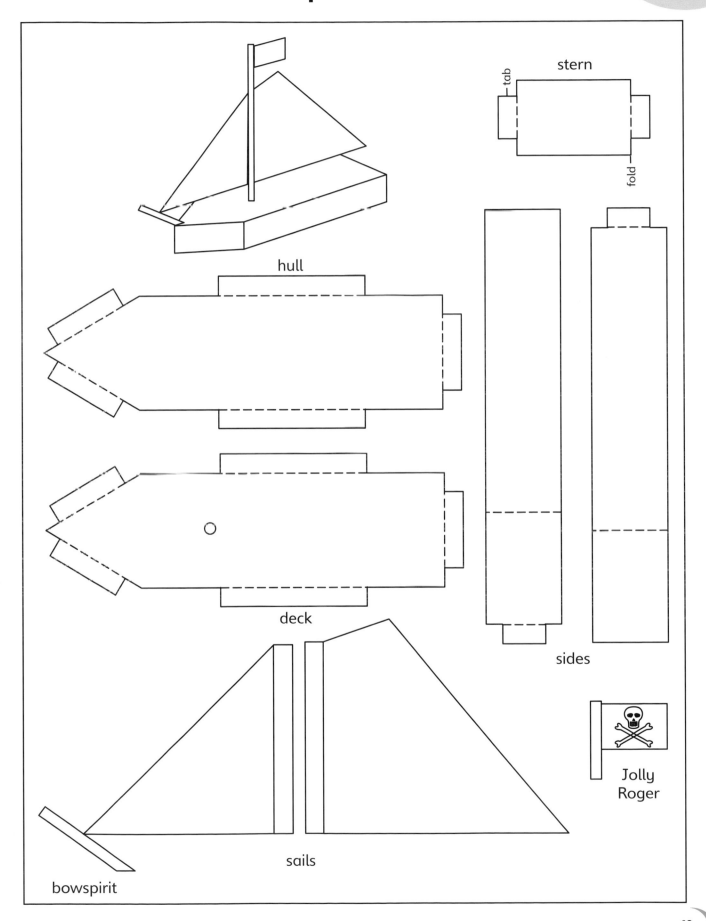

hull

deck

stern

tab

fold

sides

sails

bowspirit

Jolly Roger

The pirate crew

BACKGROUND

The pirate crew would have been made up of sailors from a variety of backgrounds, for example, the Navy or merchant ships, men who had worked on the land or runaway slaves. When pirates captured a ship, they sometimes gave the crew the option of joining them, especially if they wanted to take the ship as well as its cargo.

In the Navy, many sailors were badly treated by their captains, but pirates voted for their captains. If missions to collect booty were unsuccessful, the captain might be dismissed or even marooned. Ship rules were intended to keep the ship orderly and safe. As well as marooning, punishments might include lashings with the cat-o'-nine-tails (a whip with knotted cords). Some authorities believe that pirates did not make people walk the plank and that the idea is a work of fiction.

Pirate crews varied in the way that they were organised, usually depending on size, and often the members would do, or deputise, several jobs. The quartermaster or first mate could deputise for the captain. A bosun might have supervised several jobs. One of the sailors might have also served as the cook. If a ship had no surgeon, care of wounded pirates (and amputation) would be carried out by the carpenter or cook. While studying this theme you might like to introduce ideas for pirate costumes if you are planning a Pirate Day. Pirates wore woolly hats, bandannas, neckerchiefs, loose shirts and waistcoats. Baggy trousers which ended just below the knee were comfortable for most tasks on the ships. The captain and others with authority often wore finer clothes, such as three-cornered hats, long coats, silk shirts and shoes with buckles – often stolen.

THE CONTENTS
Lesson 1 (Ages 5–7)
Meet the pirates

The children look at some coloured pictures of pirates then colour in the clothes of the pirates on the photocopiable. They listen to information about different pirates, then try to identify them. They can cut out the pirates and write their job titles on their backs.

Lesson 2 (Ages 7–9)
Who's who

The children look at the pictures of pirates on page 21 and identify them from information on page 22. They read the short accounts of each one and match the account to the pirate. They then make a book about the pirate crew.

Lesson 3 (Ages 9–11)
Rules for the crew

The children look at a picture of a pirate crew on deck on page 23 and identify each pirate using information on page 22. They look at the code of rules that the pirates have drawn up and discuss whether they could make any better ones.

Notes on photocopiables
Meet the pirates (page 21)

This sheet features cards to colour in and stand up as simple models. The pirates are: 1) captain; 2) quartermaster; 3) first mate; 4) bosun; 5) gunner; 6) sailor; 7) cook; 8) powder monkey; 9) cabin boy; 10) female pirate.

Who's who? (page 22)

This sheet provides descriptions and job titles to match with the pictures on page 21.

Rules for the crew (page 23)

This picture of pirates on deck helps to set the scene. A set of rules based on those actually used by pirates is included for discussion.

PHOTOGRAPH © PETER ROWE, MODEL SHIP AND FIGURE © EARLY LEARNING CENTRE

HOT TOPICS Pirates

Lesson 1 Meet the pirates

Resources and preparation
- Each child or group will need: page 21 copied onto card, reference pictures of pirates, coloured pencils, scissors. Collect cardboard boxes and other materials to make model galleons about 40–45cm long. You will also need page 22 (for teacher use). This lesson can be adapted as part of your Pirate Day.

What to do
- Show the children the pictures of the pirates and talk about their clothes.
- Ask the children what they think pirates did and be prepared for lots of answers about capturing treasure!
- Tell the children that pirates were not always attacking other ships. They had to sail to find them and it could take days or even weeks before they located one. During this time the pirates had to look after their ship and prepare it for action. Tell the children that many pirates had special jobs in the running of the pirate ship.
- Show the children the pictures of pirates and let them colour in their pirate crews on page 21.
- Tell the children to cut out the cards and bend the tabs so that the crew members can stand up.

- Ask the children to hold up each picture in turn as you begin to read the information on page 22. After you and the children have considered three or four of the crew, ask them what they can remember about what they have heard.
- Repeat the point above until you have talked about the full crew.
- Ask the children which member of the crew they would like to be. (leave out the female pirate to avoid all the girls voting for her.) Collect the data and display it as a pictogram.

Extension
If you have made the galleon for Theme 1, produce it again and ask the children what they could use to make a model galleon large enough for their pirate crews (it needs to be about the same scale as the people in the pictures). Look for answers about using boxes and have a few available to consider how they could be arranged to make a ship.

Ask what other materials could be used and make some large galleons for the pirate crews.

PHOTOGRAPH © PETER ROWE

PHOTOGRAPH © ANDREA LEWIS

AGES 5–7

Objectives
- To learn the job titles of the different members of the pirate crew.
- To learn about the jobs of the different crew members.

Subject references
English
- Sustain concentration, (NC: KS1 En1 2a)
- Remember specific points that interest them. (NC: KS1 En1 2b)
- Use adventurous and wide-ranging vocabulary, (NC: KS1 En3 1a)
- Attempt unfamiliar words. (NC: KS1 En3 2a)

Mathematics
- Use simple charts to classify and organise information. (NC: KS1 Ma2 5a)

ICT
- Investigate different ways that information can be presented. (NC: KS1 ICT 5a)

Design and technology
- Generate ideas by drawing on their own and other people's experiences, (NC: KS1 1a)
- Talk about their ideas. (NC: KS1 1c)

Lesson 2 Who's who?

PHOTOGRAPH © PETER ROWE

AGES 7–9

Objectives
● To learn the job titles of the different members of the pirate crew.
● To learn about the jobs of the different crew members.
● To make a book about the pirate crew.

Subject references
English
● Identify the use and effect of specialist vocabulary.
(NC: KS2 En2 5a)
Design and technology
● Generate ideas for products after thinking about who will use them and what they will be used for.
(NC: KS2 1a)
● Select appropriate techniques for making the product.
(NC: KS2 2a)
Mathematics
● Construct frequency tables.
(NC: KS2 Ma4 2b)
● Represent data as a bar chart.
(NC: KS2 Ma4 2c)

Resources and preparation
● Each child or group will need: photocopies of pages 21 and 22, reference pictures of pirates, scissors, glue, paper, coloured pencils. This lesson can be adapted as part of your Pirate Day.

Starter
● Show the children some pictures of pirates. Ask the children what they think pirates did, and be prepared for answers about attacking ships and capturing treasure.
● Tell the children that for much of their time, pirates had to sail in order to find ships to attack. They would often be at sea for days or even weeks before they found one. Ask the children what they think the crew would have had to do during that time.
● Steer the conversation onto the running of a ship and keeping it safe; the need to know where you are going, the need to cook and ration out food, the need to trim the sails (set them up to catch the wind) and take them down again, and so on. The idea here is to encourage the children to step back from thoughts of swashbuckling and to see the pirates as real sailors doing a real job keeping their ship sound and safe at sea.

What to do
● Tell the children that every person in the pirate crew had a different job and that many of the jobs have special names. See if the children can suggest any and confirm or introduce roles such as the captain, bosun, first mate and powder monkey.
● Tell the children they are going to find out more about these jobs and give out copies of pages 21 and 22.
● Tell the children they can identify the pirates on page 21 by looking at the information at the bottom of page 22. Explain to the children that when they identify a pirate, they should look at its number and write it down on page 22 in the box next to the appropriate name. For example, the captain is number 1, so *1* should be written in the box next to the text for captain on page 22.
● When the children have matched the pictures and text they should cut them out and place each picture with its text.
● Tell the children that they are going to make a pirate book and ask them about the ways they think they could do it. When you have approved their suggestions, let the children stick down their pictures and descriptions to compile their books.

Differentiation

• Less confident learners could stick each picture on a piece of paper together with its appropriate text, then stick the pages together to make their book. They could design and make a front cover for their book.

• More confident learners might like to redraw and colour each picture on a separate page and write or stick the text underneath. They could use devices such as a window on a page where a pirate on the next page can also be seen.

Assessment

The children can be assessed on the quality of their books. They can also be assessed on their knowledge of pirates in discussion in the Plenary.

Plenary

Ask questions such as:
Why did the captain have to be a good leader?
Who were the people who looked after the cannons?

Who worked in the galley?
What job might a bosun have done?
Ask the children which member of the crew they would like to be. (Leave out the pirate woman to avoid all the girls voting for her.) Collect the data and ask the children to present it as a bar graph. If you are planning a Pirate Day, you may like to discuss pirate clothes to close the lesson.

Outcomes

• The children learn that there are different jobs in a pirate crew.

• The children can make a book to display information about a pirate crew.

Did you know?
Pirates ate biscuits called hardtack, which had weevils in them.

Lesson 3 Rules for the crew

Objectives
- To learn the names of the different roles in the pirate crew.
- To learn about the jobs of the different crew members.
- To learn about the rules by which pirates lived when on ship.
- To compare ideas about how pirates lived with the way pirates really did run their lives.

Subject references
English
- Make contributions relevant to the topic and take turns in discussion.
(NC: KS2 En1 3a)
- Identify the use and effect of specialist vocabulary.
(NC: KS2 En2 5a)
History
- Find out about people from a range of sources.
(NC: KS2 4a)
- Britain and the wider world in Tudor times.
(NC: KS2 10)

Resources and preparation
- In a large space, mark out a ship about ten metres long. Each child or group will need paper and pencils and copies of pages 22 and 23. This lesson can be adapted as part of your Pirate Day.

What to do
- Ask the children to sit inside the shape of the ship you have marked out and tell them to imagine that they are a pirate crew sailing in search of treasure. What would they need in order to stay at sea for several weeks? (Food and water, for example.)
- What tasks would need to be done in order to sail their ship successfully? Look for answers about electing a leader, dividing up the jobs such as setting the sails, navigating, looking out for ships, cooking, maintenance.
- Ask the children what they would do if one of their crew stole from another pirate or started a fight.
- The discussion should conclude that there should be some division of labour, a chain of command and perhaps some rules concerning bad behaviour. Ask the children to write down the jobs and

rules they come up with.
- Now issue pages 22 and 23. Ask the children to identify the pirates in the picture on page 23 from the information at the bottom of page 22.
- Let them read about the job of each pirate then, as a group, assess how close their organisation was to that of real pirates.
- Repeat the above task for the rules.

Extension
Tell the children that two coins that featured in pirate treasure were the *pieces of eight* (a silver coin that could be cut into eight pieces) and a gold coin called a *doubloon*. Ask the children to imagine that they are ordinary sailors entitled to a share of the treasure and that their share is one hundred doubloons each. How would they feel about the captain getting 150 doubloons and the quartermaster, bosun and gunner getting 100 doubloons? If they were the captain, quartermaster, bosun or gunner would they expect to get more than the ordinary seamen? What might happen if the captain and the other officers got much more?

ILLUSTRATION © LASZLO VERES/BEEHIVE ILLUSTRATION

Theme 2 Meet the pirates

fold

Theme 2 Who's who?

☐ **Bosun**
There were a few bosuns on each ship. Each had a special job. One was in charge of crew working the decks. Another was in charge of raising and lowering the anchor. A third was responsible for the rigging.

☐ **Cabin boy**
The cabin boy was a servant of the captain. He ran errands and took messages from the captain to other members of the crew.

☐ **Captain**
The crew chose the captain. The captain was brave and a very good fighter. He would make his men feel brave so they would fight with him to capture ships and take cargoes. The captain also knew how to sail the ship to the places the crew wanted to go.

☐ **Cook**
The cook worked in the galley making meals for the rest of the crew.

☐ **Female pirate**
A few pirate ships had a pirate woman on board. She helped to run the ship and would fight in the battles.

☐ **First mate**
The first mate was the captain's deputy. He could do all the captain's jobs and, if the captain was injured or killed, would take command of the ship and lead the crew in battle.

☐ **Gunner**
A gunner could aim a cannon on target. It took many years to learn how to fire a cannon. He would help other pirates to fire the guns when they attacked another ship.

☐ **Powder monkey**
A powder monkey was a boy of about 12 years old. He helped the pirates fire the cannons.

☐ **Quartermaster**
The quartermaster shared out the food, allocated the tasks and divided the booty. He decided how disobedient pirates would be punished.

☐ **Sailor**
A sailor did many different jobs. He would run up the rigging and trim the sails, and clean the decks.

How to recognise the crew members
The powder monkey is dressed in rags. The bosun has a hat and coat with two idenitical rows of buttons. The captain has a hook. The cabin boy wears a hat and coat. The quartermaster has a hat and sword. The female pirate has an axe. The gunner has a wooden leg. The first mate has a bandanna, cutlass and a coat. The cook has a bald head and a beard. The sailor wears a woolly hat and earrings.

Theme 2 Rules for the crew

1. The captain will have a one-and-a-half share of all booty. The quartermaster, bosun and gunner shall have one-and-a-quarter shares. Everyone else shall have one share.

2. Anyone who withholds a secret from the crew, or attempts to flee will be marooned with a pistol, shot, powder and a bottle of water.

3. Anyone who steals from another crew member will be marooned, as above, or shot.

4. Anyone who strikes another person as part of a disagreement will receive 39 strokes of the cat-o'-nine-tails.

5. Anyone who takes a lit candle below decks without casing it in a lantern will receive 39 strokes of the cat-o'-nine-tails.

6. Anyone who does not keep their weapons clean and ready for battle, or does not perform their duties in the running of the ship may not receive a share of the booty, and may receive further punishment, as decided by the captain and crew.

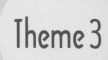

Under sail

BACKGROUND

Sailing ships were powered by the wind. The pushing force of the wind against the sails drove the ship through the water. A ship's hull was streamlined – it had a pointed bow from which the sides curved outwards and then back inwards a little towards the stern. This shape allowed the water to pass smoothly around the ship and keep water resistance low.

When pirates attacked another ship they aimed to disable it rather than sink it. They would fire into the sails to tear holes in them and at the masts to break them and bring down the sails.

As well as being able to travel at speed it was important for pirates to be able to navigate. They stole charts from captured ships and used a compass to follow directions, using the magnetic nature of the Earth. A compass was placed on the chart and the chart was moved until the north on the chart pointed in the same direction as the compass.

THE CONTENTS
Lesson 1 (Ages 5–7)
Testing sails

The children attach sails of different sizes to model ships and gently blow on them to compare how well they catch the wind and move along.

Lesson 2 (Ages 7–9)
Sails and directions

The children make model ships with sails of different sizes and gently blow on them to compare how effective the sails are. They also make a ship which has a damaged mast and tattered sail after a pirate attack and compare how it moves with the undamaged ships. The children also learn how to use a compass to find directions.

Lesson 3 (Ages 9–11)
Plotting a course

The children practise directions and use a map to plot a course.

Notes on photocopiables
Testing sails (page 29)

The sheet features sails of different sizes for the children to cut out and stick to a straw and place on a model ship. There are spaces for the children to write down their observations about the ships' movements.

Sails and directions (page 30)

This sheet shows how cannon fire could damage sails and masts, and a suggestion is shown of how to make a damaged ship to test. The second section of the sheet presents the points of the compass and has space for recording compass-point observations.

Plotting a course (page 31)

A map is provided here for the children to use to plot a course.

PHOTOGRAPH © LOTUS HEAD, STOCK.XCHNG

Lesson 1 Testing sails

Resources and preparation
• Each child or group will need a copy of page 29, four straws, scissors, sticky tape, a lump of plasticine about two centimetres across, four model hulls (see below), a large tray of water, a balloon inflator or large plastic syringe.

Make the model hull in the following way. Take a clean plastic bottle (about 7.5cm long - a yogurt drink bottle is ideal), and cut it in two lengthways. This makes two hulls. Fold a 4cm-square piece of kitchen foil over the half neck of the bottle and fold it up to make the bow of the ship (see the illustration on page 29).

This lesson can be adapted as part of your Pirate Day.

What to do
• Ask the children how they think the size of the sails may affect the movement of a ship. Explain that the larger the sail, the faster and further the ship will travel. Tell the children that they are going to test this idea with an experiment.
• Give out copies of page 29 and go through the stages of making the ship. Point out that one ship has no sail, just a mast.

• Let the children take their time to assemble four ships.
• Ask the children to launch each ship at the edge of the shallow tray and use a balloon inflator or large plastic syringe to blow gently on the sails.
• Tell the children to make several attempts at sailing each ship, then write a simple report in the spaces on the sheet (or on the back of the sheet if their handwriting is large).
• Encourage the children to discuss their reports and present their conclusions.

Extension
Explain to the children that when pirates attacked a ship they did not want to sink it, because that would take the treasure to the bottom of the sea. Ask the children how pirates might have stopped or slowed a target ship. Take a ship with a large sail and say that you are a pirate attacking it. Cut some pieces of sail away as shown at the bottom of page 30, bend the mast a little to show that it has also been damaged. Let two children explore how the damaged ship sails compared with an undamaged ship.

AGES 5–7

Objectives
• To assemble simple model ships.
• To make observations and record them.
• To draw conclusions.

Subject references
Science
• Recognise when a test or comparison is unfair. (NC: KS1 Sc1 2d)
• Communicate what happened in writing. (NC: KS1 Sc1 2g)
• Make simple comparisons and identify simple patterns or associations. (NC: KS1 Sc1 2h)
Design and technology
• Assemble, join and combine materials. (NC: KS1 2d)

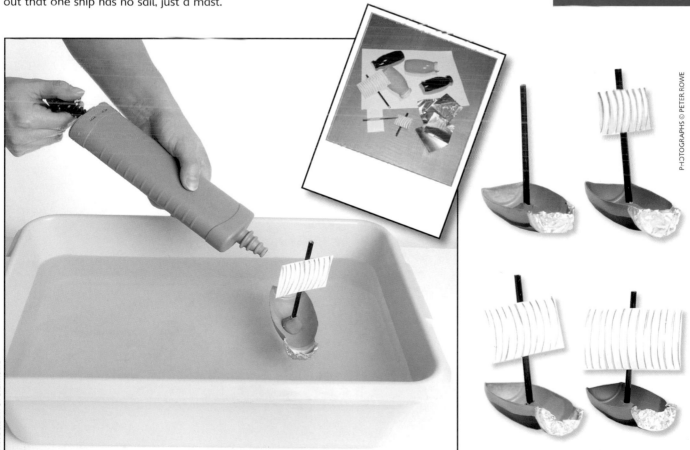

PHOTOGRAPH © PETER ROWE

PHOTOGRAPHS © PETER ROWE

Lesson 2 Sails and directions

AGES 7–9

Objectives
● To assemble simple model ships.
● To make observations and record them.
● To draw conclusions.
● To learn how to use a compass to find directions.

Subject references
Science
● Make a fair test, or comparison by changing one factor and observing or measuring the effect while keeping the other factors the same.
(NC: KS2 Sc1 2d)
● Check observations and measurements by repeating them where appropriate.
(NC: KS2 Sc1 2g)
● Learn about forces of attraction and repulsion.
(NC: KS2 Sc4 2a)
● Learn about air resistance.
(NC: KS2 Sc4 2c)
Design and technology
● Measure, mark out, cut and shape a range of materials, and assemble, join and combine materials accurately.
(NC: KS2 2d)

Resources and preparation
● Each child or group will need a copy of page 29 and of page 30, four straws, scissors, sticky tape, a lump of plasticine about two centimetres across, four hulls made from small bottles cut lengthways (see page 25, but leaving off the foil bows for the children to add), four squares of kitchen foil (4cm square), a large tray of water, a balloon inflator or large plastic syringe, a ruler for more confident learners, a compass. This lesson can be adapted as part of your Pirate Day.

Starter
● Ask the children what power the pirates used to move their ships. Look for an answer that mentions the power of the wind.
● Ask the children how the ship could use the power of the wind. Look for an answer about sails 'catching' the wind. If the children have studied friction and air resistance, recall that learning here. They might have studied air resistance as a force that slows things down. Explain that here it is the air resistance of the sails that catches the wind and allows the ship to be pushed forwards. If the children ask about how friction affects the ship, tell them that there is friction between the hull and the water, water resistance, but this force is kept to a minimum by the ship's hull having a streamlined shape.

● Now consider how pirates might have found their way around the seas once they had got their ship moving. Look for an answer about using a compass. Tell the children that in this lesson they are going to investigate sails and find directions with a compass.

What to do
● Issue page 29 and demonstrate the stages in attaching a bow to the hull, then ask the children to add bows to their mini-ships. Suggest that the children float their hulls in the trays of water to make sure they are watertight.
● Go through the making stages with the children. Point out that they will need to make one ship with a mast but no sail to test the effect of a sail on a ship.
● When the children have assembled their ships, ask them to test their sails by blowing gently with a balloon inflator or large syringe. Make sure that they repeat the experiments and record their observations or measurements.
● Issue page 30 and examine the picture of a pirate ship attacking a galleon. Draw attention to the damaged mast and sails and compare this with the picture on the right, which shows a suggestion for modelling a damaged ship.
● Ask the children take their ship with the largest sail and to damage the sail and mast as if the ship had been attacked by pirates.

PHOTOGRAPH © PETER ROWE

HOT TOPICS Pirates

They may cut their sail and bend the mast as in the picture or decide upon their own damage.

● Let the children sail their damaged ship and compare how well it sails now with the way it sailed before it was damaged.

● Move on to discuss direction-finding, and hand out the compasses. Tell the children to place their compass in the centre of the square on the sheet and let the needle settle in a North-South direction.

● Then ask the children to move the paper carefully under the compass until North and South are in line with the directions pointed by the compass needle.

● Tell the children to select ten objects around them and write down the direction for them from the compass.

Differentiation

● Less confident learners may record their observations qualitatively, for example: *The ship without a sail covered the least distance.*

● More confident learners could measure how far each ship sailed. They could repeat their experiment and construct a table in which to record their results. Encourage them to draw a conclusion from their data.

Assessment

The children can be assessed by the way they made their ships and the way they tested them, as well as in their recordings of observations and measurements. They can be assessed on how accurately they can use a compass.

Plenary

● Review the results of the children's experiments on the ships. Ask them to reflect on how the crew of a damaged ship would feel when they could not escape from the pirates.

● Check the directions of the various classroom objects the children have found with their compasses and agree which parts of the classroom face in which direction.

● Now ask the children to imagine that the classroom is the inside of a pirate ship which has changed direction, to help them realise the importance of the compass on a ship.

Outcomes

● The children can make model ships.

● The children can perform experiments to test different sails.

● The children can find directions using a compass.

Lesson 3 Plotting a course

AGES 9–11

Objectives
● To appreciate the effect of sails on the movement of ships.
● To know the eight points of the compass.
● To plot a course following directions.

Subject references
Science
● Make a fair test, or comparison by changing one factor and observing or measuring the effect while keeping the other factors the same.
(NC: KS2 Sc1 2d)
● Check observations and measurements by repeating them.
(NC: KS2 Sc1 2g)
● Learn about forces of attraction and repulsion.
(NC: KS2 Sc4 2a)
● Learn about air resistance.
(NC: KS2 Sc4 2c)
Design and technology
● Measure, mark out, cut and shape a range of materials, and assemble, join and combine materials accurately.
(NC: KS2 2d)

Resources and preparation
● Each child or group will need a copy of page 31, two straws, scissors, sticky tape, a lump of plasticine about two centimetres across, two hulls made as on page 25, (but without the bows), two pieces of foil 4cm square, a large tray of water, a balloon inflator or large plastic syringe, a ruler, a compass, a pair of compasses with a pencil in place (to serve as dividers). This lesson can be adapted as part of your Pirate Day.

What to do
● Issue page 31 and materials and show the children the items needed to make two model ships. Briefly describe how to make the ships.
● Let the children make two ships with different-sized sails.
● Ask the children to find out how the size of the sails affects the movement of the ships.
● Explain that pirates would shoot at the sails and masts of target ships. Ask the children to cut the sails and/or bend the mast of the ship with the larger sail and test how its movement is affected.
● Ask the children to put a compass in the centre of the square on page 31. When the

needle has settled, move the paper beneath it until North and South are aligned.
● Let the children find the direction of objects around the room.
● The children could try and make each ship sail in a direction of their choosing and assess how accurately it stays on course.

Extension
● Tell the children that sailors used a chart, a compass and a pair of dividers to set a course. Demonstrate how to use the dividers with the scale. Tell the children to start their galleon at point A and follow the directions to B. A pirate ship is moored at P1, ready to sail to attack. When the galleon is in sight of the port the children must decide whether to take a route close to the pirates but with more chance of being seen or further from the pirates with less chance of being seen.
● Then tell the children to sail from A to pick up marooned sailors at M and take them to Port C. There are pirate ships at P2 and P3, so the children must plot a course which offers the least chance of their ship being spotted.

Did you know?
Pirates call a telescope a 'bring 'em near'.

PHOTOGRAPH © 2007 JUPITERIMAGES CORPORATION

PHOTOGRAPH © PETER ROWE

Theme 3 **Testing sails**

1. Cut out the three sails.

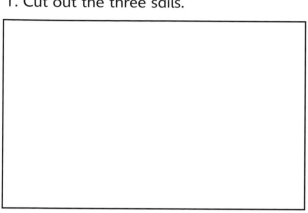

2. Fix the foil to the front of the hull to make a bow.

A 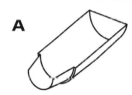   **B** 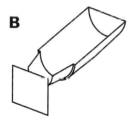   **C**    **D**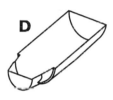

3. Make the mast and assemble your ship.

A. Cut the straws to make four masts 10cm long.

B. Stick each sail to a mast.

C. Put a small lump of plasticine on the base of each mast.

D. Attach the mast to the hull.

   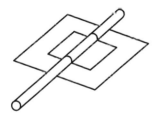   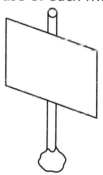   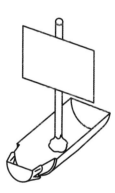

How well did it sail?

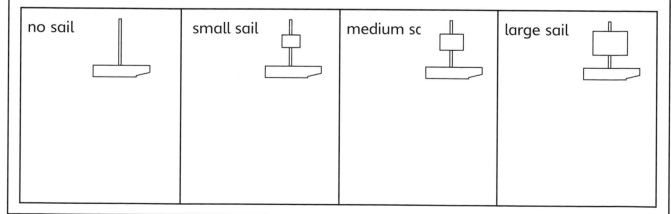

no sail	small sail	medium sc	large sail

Theme 3 Sails and directions

Your ship has been attacked! Compare how well it sails now with how well it sailed before being damaged.

E

F

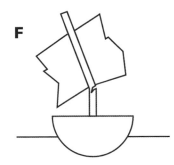

Which direction?	
Object	Compass direction

Place your compass on the compass square below. Move the sheet until north is in line with the compass needle.

NW   N   NE

W   E

SW   S   SE

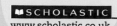
Theme 3 Plotting a course

Sailing to a course

Use a pair of dividers with the scale below to plot this course:

Directions

12 miles NE, 3 miles E, 11 miles N, 6 miles W.

Choose the next course: 7 miles SW or, 5 miles W and 4 miles S.

0 1 2 3 4 5 6 7 8 9 10 11 12 13 14 miles

NW	N	NE
W	O	E
SW	S	SE

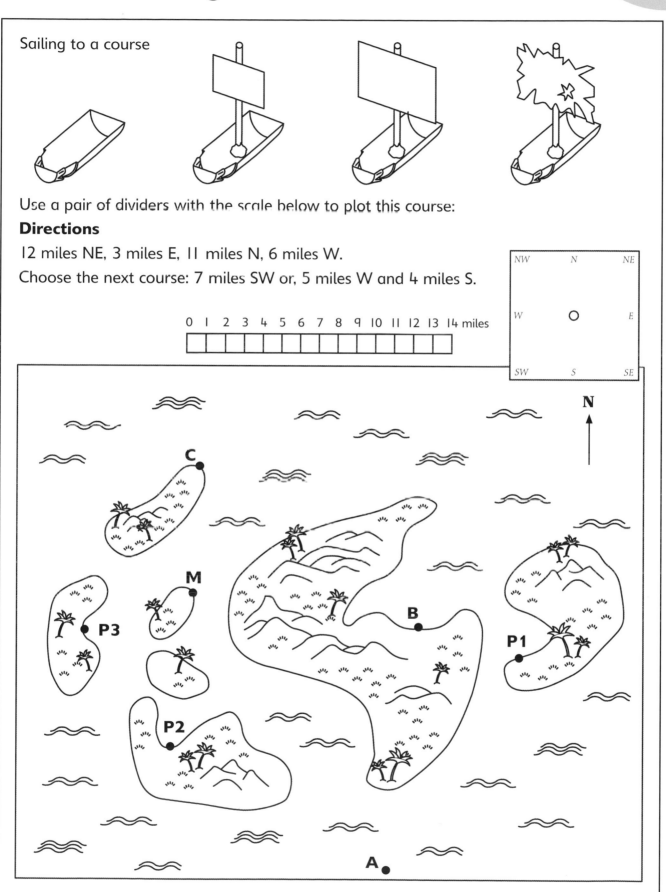

Life on board

BACKGROUND

This theme helps children to appreciate that a sailing ship is a complex mode of transport, and pirates, as all sailors, had to know all its parts and how they worked. Ships were made watertight by caulking – pushing unravelled rope coated in tar into the cracks between the planks. The decks were swabbed to keep the planks wet and swollen to prevent any further water entering the hull. Some water would still enter the ship and gather at its lowest part called the bilge. The water could be removed from here with pumps.

On a ship, a day is divided into *watches*, marked by the ringing of a bell. There are seven watches:

- Middle watch: midnight to 4.00am (0000–0400)
- Morning watch: 4.00am – 8.00am (0400–0800)
- Forenoon watch: 8.00am – noon (0800–1200)
- Afternoon watch: noon – 4.00pm (1200–1600)
- First dog watch: 4.00pm – 6.00pm (1600–1800)
- Second dog watch: 6.00pm – 8.00pm (1800–2000)
- First watch: 8.00pm – midnight (2000–0000).

The sailors on watch steer the ship, trim the sails and keep a look out.

A selection of nautical terms is included on page 38. You might like to add to it with others from throughout the book.

THE CONTENTS
Lesson 1 (Ages 5–7)
Inside a ship
The children examine the inside of a pirate ship to identify the different parts. They look at how the masts fit onto the ship.

Lesson 2 (Ages 7–9)
Bells and pirate talk
The children look at the terms used by a pirate and read about one example of its use. They then make their own accounts.

Lesson 3 (Ages 9–11)
Masts, sails and rigging
The children identify the different parts of a ship. They make a complete labelled picture of a ship.

Notes on photocopiables
Inside the ship (page 37)
This is a simple illustration of the inside of a ship. The parts are: A – figurehead, B – cannon, C – forecastle, D – hatch, E – main deck, F – hold, G – lower deck, H – captain's cabin, I – galley, J – officers' cabins, K – wheel, L – capstan, M – rudder, N – keel, O – bilge.

Talking pirate (page 38)
The sheet shows some terms used by pirates. The pirate is saying: 'Hello friend. Are you a new pirate? Are you frightened? I am a pirate and I am going on a pirate trip. Do not upset me because I show no mercy.'

Masts, sails and rigging (page 39)
These are the sails, mast and rigging of the ship on page 37. The parts are: 1) bowsprit; 2) jib sail; 3) foremast shrouds; 4) foremast main sail; 5) foremast crow's nest; 6) foremast top sail; 7) foremast banner, 8) main mast shrouds; 9) mainmast main sail; 10) mainmast crow's nest; 11) mainmast top sail; 12) mainmast banner; 13) poop deck; 14) swivel gun; 15) lantern; 16) mizzen mast ratlines; 17) lateen sail; 18) gaff; 19) mizzen mast crow's nest; 20) mizzen mast topsail; 21) mizzen mast main sail; 22) mizzen mast banner. This list should be written on the board to be used with the photocopiable. (A shroud is a vertical rope, a ratline is a horizontal rope connecting the shrouds).

PHOTOGRAPH © NICOLAS SALES, STOCK.XCHNG

Lesson 1 Inside a ship

Resources and preparation
● Each child or group will need a copy of page 37, scissors, glue, paper and pencils.

What to do
● Ask the children to imagine that they are pirates about to join a ship. The ship is their home and they should learn all its different parts.
● Issue copies of page 37 and explain to the children that they are going to learn what the labelled parts are.
● Ask the children to cut out the labels ready to fix them to the picture of the ship.
● Talk about each part in turn and ask the children to identify it. For example:
The figurehead is at the front of the ship.
The cannon is like a large gun.
The forecastle is where most of the pirates sleep.
The hatch is a covered opening in a deck.
The main deck is the top deck.
The lower deck is below the main deck.
The wheel is near the back of the ship.
The capstan has four arms and is turned to raise the anchor (the anchor is not shown).
The captain's cabin is at the back of the ship.

The officers' cabins are next to the captain's cabin.
The hold contains barrels and boxes.
The rudder is at the back of the ship.
The keel is at the bottom of the ship.
The bilge is below the hold.
The galley is where food is cooked.
● Prompt the children to imagine moving round the ship. Ask them to follow a path on page 37 with their fingers as you speak. Start in the forecastle where they are asleep in their hammocks. They then come out on the main deck and scrub it to keep it clean; go down the steps by the wheel to the galley for breakfast. Then they go to the hatch in the lower deck and drop into the hold and inspect the bilge to see if it is full of water. If the bilge starts to fill with water they have to pump it out.

Extension
Give out copies of page 39. Show the children how it can be joined to page 37 then let them glue them together. Ignore the numbers provided for the older children and write on the board: *foremast, main mast, mizzen mast, rat lines, poop deck* and *swivel guns*. Ask the children to copy the words as labels and attach them to the picture.

AGES 5–7

Objectives
● To learn about the parts of a pirate ship.
● To listen and use what is heard to answer a question.

Subject references
English
● Sustain concentration, (NC: KS1 En1 2a)
● Ask questions to clarify their understanding. (NC: KS1 En1 2e)
● Write familiar words and attempt unfamiliar ones. (NC: KS1En3 2a)
History
● Identify differences between ways of life at different times. (NC: KS1 2b)

PHOTOGRAPHS © ANDREA LEWIS

Lesson 2 Bells and pirate talk

AGES 7–9

Objectives
● To become aware that a routine was needed on ship for her crew to survive.
● To construct sentences in the style of 'pirate talk'.

Subject references
Mathematics
● Read the time from analogue and digital 12- and 24-hour clocks, use units of time and know the relationship between them.
(NC: KS2 Ma34d)
English
● Identify different ways of constructing sentences and their effects.
(NC: KS2 En2 4b)
● Respond imaginatively, drawing on the whole text and other reading.
(NC: KS2 En2 4h)
History
● Find out about people from an appropriate range of sources.
(NC: KS2 4a)

Resources and preparation
● Each child or group will need a photocopy of page 38, an analogue and/or digital watch, a bell. You might like to read from a copy of *Treasure Island*. If this lesson is used in the morning, you could keep the bells ringing all day! The lesson can be adapted to form part of your Pirate Day.

Starter
Tell the children that the 24 hours of a day on a ship are grouped into watches. You might want to write them on the board – see page 32. Explain that the dog watches break up the time period into an uneven number of watches, which allowed sailors to have some flexibility in the hours they worked. For example, certain sailors could be on first dog watch, then first watch, or second dog watch, then middle watch. On the following day they could be on a different dog watch which would lead to them working on other watches after having some time off for sleep.

What to do
● Tell the children that the watches were divided into half-hour periods, and after each half hour a bell was rung in the following way:
After half an hour – one bell.
After one hour – two bells.
After one and half hours – two bells, pause then one bell.
After two hours – two bells, pause then two bells.
After two and half hours – two bells, pause, two bells then one bell.
After three hours – two bells, pause, two bells, pause, two bells.
After three and a half hours – two bells, pause, two bells, pause, two bells then one bell
After four hours – eight bells.
● Ask someone to tell you what the time is. Ask the children to work out how the time would be signalled in the watch system and prepare to ring the bell appropriately on the half hour. Let them continue this practice throughout the day.

ILLUSTRATION © LASZLO VERES/BEEHIVE ILLUSTRATION

Did you know?

Pirates kept pet monkeys and parrots to sell when they went ashore.

- Some children may wish to continue ringing bells at home! They need to know that in the first dog watch the pattern is as for the first two hours of a normal watch. In the second dog watch the bell pattern for the end of the half hour periods is one, two, three then eight.

- A good way to introduce pirate talk is by reading from *Treasure Island* Chapter 8 'At the sign of the Spy Glass', starting at the sixth paragraph and reading the conversation between Jim, Long John Silver and Tom Morgan.

- Ask the children to identify ways in which Long John Silver spoke differently from the way we do today. Elicit the unusual vocabulary he used: terms such as *score,* meaning *payment; dead eye* – a wooden block used to connect rigging to the sides of the ship; and *keel haul,* which was a pirate punishment where a sailor was dragged under the hull and usually drowned.

- Tell the children that you have a glossary of pirate terms for them and that included in it are *swab* and *lubber,* mentioned in the *Treasure Island* extract. Give out copies of page 38 and let the children find the words.

- Read through the paragraph explaining how pirates talked. Let the children enjoy practising some of the glossary terms, and then ask them to translate what the pirate is saying at the bottom of the sheet.

Differentiation

- Give less confident learners extra support and practice in understanding the time periods in analogue and digital form. They might also need help in reading the words on page 38.

- Encourage more confident learners to divide up a typical day into watches and identify the watches when they are asleep, having meals and coming and going from school. They might also be able to construct a dialogue in pirate talk and perform it.

Assessment

The children can be assessed on the ease with which they can tell the time in analogue and digital format, the accuracy in the way they translate the pirate's speech and the sentences they construct in 'pirate talk'.

Plenary

Let the children make up their own sentences using terms in the list and following the instructions on the sheet. Ask the children to read out their sentences and challenge others to successfully translate them.

Outcomes

- The children can tell the time using analogue and digital clocks.
- They can construct sentences in the style of 'pirate talk'.
- They can translate and understand the meaning of sentences constructed in 'pirate talk'.

Lesson 3 Masts, sails and rigging

Objectives
● To learn the names of the different parts of a ship.
● To appreciate that pirates had to know a special vocabulary to find their way around a ship.

Subject references
English
● Identify the use of a specialist vocabulary. (NC: KS2 En2 5a)
History
● Britain and the wider world in Tudor times – ships and seafaring. (NC: KS2 10)

Resources and preparation
● Each child or group will need a copy of page 37 and of page 39, scissors and glue.

What to do
● Write on the board the list of terms for the parts of the masts, sails and rigging on a ship, provided in the notes on photocopiables on page 32. You might want to mix up the order of the terms to provide more of a challenge.
● Issue copies of page 39 and help the children to identify the different numbered parts. If they have already worked on Lesson 3 in Theme 1, remind them of that learning so that they can identify the masts. This should help them to get started.
● When the children have finished, issue page 37. Ask the children to cut out the labels and identify the parts of the interior of the ship. They should stick the labels in place when they have correctly identified the parts.
● Now ask the children to join pages 37 and 39 together to make a complete picture of the ship.

Extension
● The children could make a cover for the inside of the ship so that it might be used as a flap. The cover should follow the shape of the hull, show that it is made of planks and have a hole for each cannon.
● Encourage the children to envisage what it would be like to work on a pirate ship. Talk about what is involved to keep it sailing. For example, think about going up the ratlines to furl or unfurl the top sails, coming down the ratlines and spending time in the crow's nest on lookout duty, coming down the ratlines again and going down the steps to help the gunner, then going down the hatch into the hold and pumping out water that has collected in the bilge.

Theme 4 Inside a ship

figurehead	forecastle	main deck	wheel	cannon	captain's cabin
hatch	lower deck	capstan	galley	hold	officers' cabins
lantern	bilge	keel	rudder		

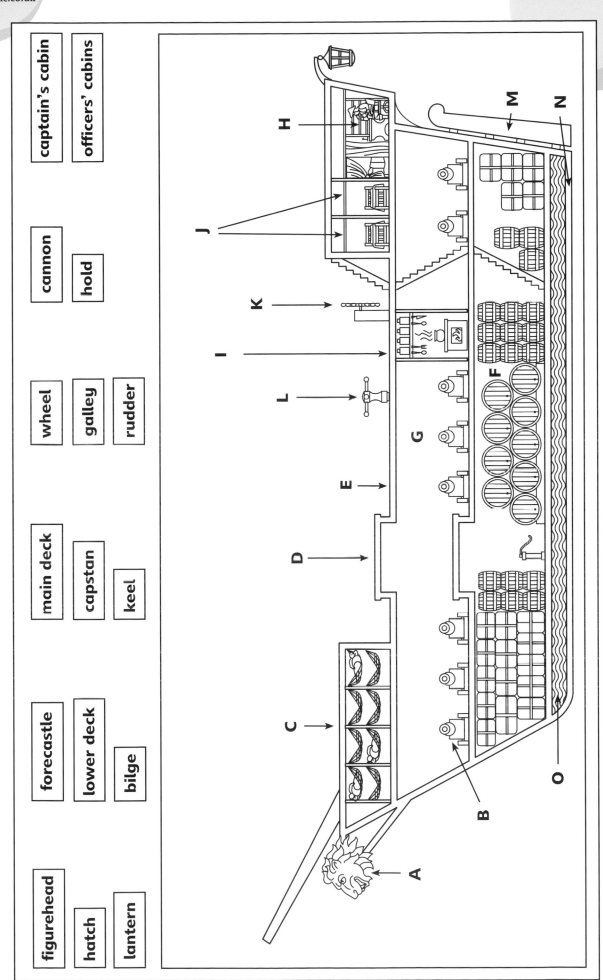

Pirate times

BACKGROUND

Piracy has taken place almost as long as people have carried goods in ships, and it still goes on today in parts of the world. It occurred in the times of the Ancient Greeks and Romans, and the Vikings might be considered as pirates too.

From the 17th century, some of the rulers of certain countries began enlisting the use of pirates or brave men by giving them Letters of Marque. These were permissions to attack enemy ships, capture them and take their cargoes. This booty was then shared out between the government of the country and the possessor of the Letter of Marque, (who was known as a privateer) and his men. Some privateers who became experts at capturing foreign vessels became out-and-out pirates and kept all the booty. The main pirate group in the Mediterranean were the Barbary corsairs who sailed along the north-African coast. Buccaneers originated in the Caribbean. They were European settlers who hunted wild cattle and pigs and smoked their meat in devices called 'boucans'. The smoked meat was sold to sailors on passing ships; hence the name 'buccaneers'.

THE CONTENTS
Lesson 1 (Ages 5–7)
Famous pirates

The children learn about some famous pirates. This lesson works best in conjunction with the pirate song in Theme 9 Lesson 1.

Lesson 2 (Ages 7–9)
Where pirates sailed

The children explore cargo routes across the oceans and shade in areas of the world where pirates were active.

Lesson 3 (Ages 9–11)
A pirate timeline

The children learn about Letters of Marque, privateers, buccaneers and corsairs. They reorder events in the past to make a timeline of piracy, and consider piracy as a crime.

Notes on photocopiables
Famous pirates (page 45)

This sheet provides information about five famous pirates and three pirate flags.

Where pirates sailed (page 46)

A map of the world is featured with the main areas where pirates were active. The children use the information to find the areas on a globe and see how far away the pirates were from the British Isles.

A Pirate timeline (page 47)

The photocopiable has a muddled-up list of events involving pirates. They need to be cut out and arranged in chronological order.

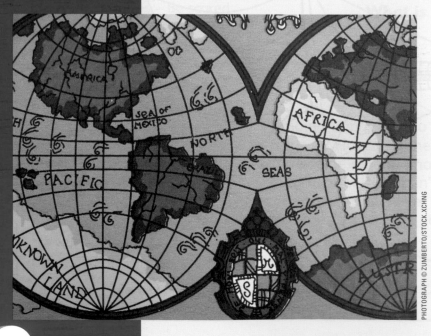

PHOTOGRAPH © ZUMBERTO/STOCK.XCHNG

Lesson 1 Famous pirates

Resources and preparation

- Each child or group will need a photocopy of page 45. You will need adult support listen to the children reading. The materials you will need to make the flags will depend on the time you wish to spend on this activity, and on the ability of the children. They could include black paper or cloth, white paper or cloth, red paper or cloth, glue, black and red felt-tipped pens. The following website is useful for generating ideas: www.kipar.org/piratical-resources/pirate-flags.html. This lesson could be used to introduce producing costumes for your Pirate Day.

What to do

- Tell the children that some of the stories they hear about pirates are not true, but there *were* real pirates and we do know some things about them.
- Issue copies of page 45 and help the children to read it. Support individuals as they read aloud in small groups.
- Now point out that the pirates sometimes had nicknames and had ships with special names too. Ask the children to think about what pirate nickname they might give themselves and what name they might like for their ship.

www.openclipart.org

- Go on to tell the children that Calico Jack was a pirate who liked to wear very fancy clothes. Ask the children how they might like to look if they were pirates.

Extension

- Point out that each pirate had his own distinctive flag. In addition to a skull and crossbones, flags also featured cutlasses, skeletons, hearts, hourglasses (indicating that time is running out) and wings (time is flying). Explain that the purpose of a Jolly Roger (pirate's flag) was to scare people so that they would surrender and not fight. This would mean that the pirates did not come to any harm and would avoid damage to either ship.
- Ask the children to design and make their own Jolly Rogers for a pirate flag display.

PHOTOGRAPH © PETER ROWE
PHOTOGRAPHS © ANDREA LEWIS

Lesson 2 Where pirates sailed

AGES 7–9

Objectives
● To identify trade routes across the oceans.
● To identify areas where pirates were active.

Subject references
Geography
● Use maps.
(NC: KS2 2c)
● Study a range of places in different parts of the world.
(NC: KS2 7b)
History
● Find out about events and people in the past.
(NC: KS2 4a)

Resources and preparation
● Each child or group will need a photocopy of page 46 and coloured pens or pencils. You will also need a class map or globe. Before the lesson, write on the board activities 1 to 11 shown in the 'What to do' section below.

Starter
● Ask the children to offer a definition of *pirate*. Look for suggestions that incorporate ideas of: taking things that do not belong to them, using violence to get their way, and using ships as a means of transport. If the children have studied the Vikings, ask them to consider whether or not Vikings were pirates. From the characteristics they have identified they should probably conclude that the Vikings were indeed pirates.
● Now tell the children that they are going to study areas of the globe in which pirates have been active in the past.

What to do
● Hand out the copies of page 46 and point out to the children that it contains information that they will need to use in the activities that follow.

Activities
● Read through the activities on the board (given below) and let the children try them on their photocopiable sheets.
1. Shade in the seas around Greece to show where Greek pirates were active.
2. Shade in the seas around Italy to show where the Roman pirates were active.
3. Shade in the seas around Britain to show where the Vikings were active.
4. Shade in the seas along the coast (the Barbary Coast) between Algiers and Tripoli to show where the corsairs were active.
5. Draw a line between Nombre de Dios and Cadiz to show the route taken by the Spanish to carry home the Inca gold.
6. Draw a line from Bristol to the Gold Coast and from there to Jamaica and back to Bristol to show the route taken by ships in the Slave Trade Triangle.
7. Draw a line from London into the Indian Ocean, then draw three lines from it: one to Bombay, one to Madras, and one to Calcutta, to show the routes taken by the cargo ships of the East India Company.
8. Shade in the South China Sea where the Chinese pirates were active.
9. Draw in the Pirate Round from the

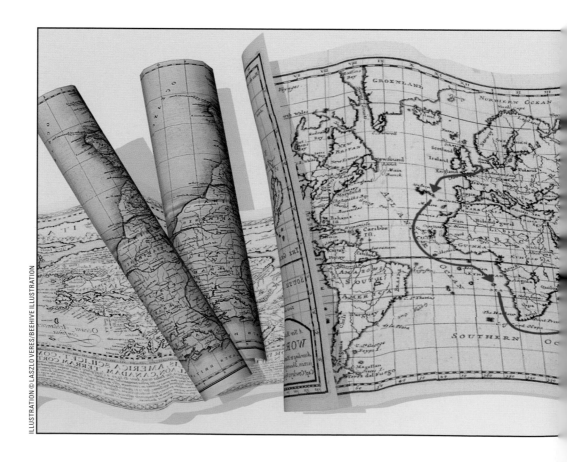

ILLUSTRATION © LASZLO VERES/BEEHIVE ILLUSTRATION

Caribbean Sea to the Gold Coast then to the Arabian Sea. This was the route taken by pirates of this area as they looked for ships to attack.

10. Where do you think many pirates hid away between North and South America? Shade this area in another colour.

11. Where do you think many pirates hid away in the Indian Ocean? Shade this area in a third colour.

Differentiation

• Less-confident readers might need help locating the places on the map. Give help with reading but encourage their visual and geographical skills.

• More-confident can look at the places on a globe and see how far around the world the pirates travelled when they sailed the Pirate Round.

Assessment

The children can be assessed on shading in the correct areas in activities 1 to 4, drawing lines to the correct points in activities 5 to 9 and judgement in selecting the Caribbean islands and Madagascar as places where pirates would hide in answer to the questions in activities 10 and 11.

Plenary

Many people go abroad on holiday. Do any of the children in the class go on holiday where pirates were once active? Popular holiday resorts are on the Spanish coast and islands such as Majorca, the Greek islands, Cyprus, Malta, the Canary Islands, the Bahamas and Florida. Let the children find these places on a map and compare their positions with the regions of pirate activity shown on the map on the photocopiable sheet.

Outcomes

• The children can mark out trade routes across the world in pirate times.

• The children can locate areas of the world where pirates were once active.

Did you know?

Pirates caught fish, seabirds and turtles to eat and raided islands for fruit and coconuts.

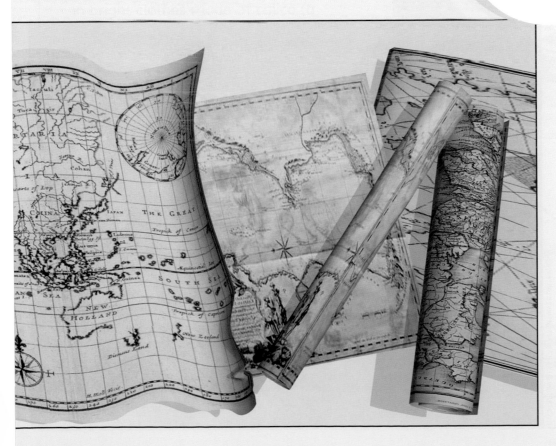

Taking the booty

BACKGROUND

When sailors put to sea they stored all their belongings in a wooden chest reinforced with strips metal at the edges, corners and across its surfaces.

When pirates went on a raid they aimed to capture booty without harming themselves or their ship. They brought their ship close to the enemy but keeping out of range of its cannons. Chain-linked cannon balls, called chain shot, were used to bring down masts, rigging and sails to stop a target ship escaping. Cannons also fired many small pieces of iron, called grapeshot.

The Jolly Roger is thought to get its name from the French *joli rouge* that describe a red flag used by pirates such as the Barbary corsairs.

Pirates are sometimes considered slaves as booty, like gold and silver. Slavery was legal in pirate times. The human suffering was terrible. Some slaves ran away and joined pirate crews.

THE CONTENTS

Lesson 1 (Ages 5–7)
Treasure chest

The children learn about pirates' chests and make a treasure chest. This lesson links to Lesson 1 in Theme 7, where the children make treasure to put in their chests.

Lesson 2 (Ages 7–9)
Pirate raids

The children look at the tactics that pirates used to capture booty. They can make their own Jolly Roger and identify the weapons used by pirates.

The Lesson 3 (Ages 9–11)
Slaves

While lessons 1 and 2 can be delivered in a light-hearted way, this lesson takes a serious look at slavery, as pirates also captured and sold slaves and some pirates *were* slaves who had escaped from their masters.

Notes on photocopiables
Treasure chest (page 53)

There are two components to the treasure chest for children to cut out and assemble. They can use the illustration to make their chests look more realistic.

Pirate raids (page 54)

There are components of pirate flags for the children to consider in designing and making their own flags. The main picture of the raid shows a range of weapons used by pirates: A) bow and arrow; B) grenade; C) cannon; D) chain shot; E) musket; F) kris; G) cutglass; H) boarding axe; I) dagger; J) pistol; K) cannon ball; L) musketoon.

Slaves (page 55)

This page provides information about the slave trade and a series of questions based on it. Answers: 3) The arrow from Africa to Jamaica; 4) 2000 manilla; 5) 160; 6) 24,000 manilla; 7) He made 22,000 manilla profit. Some children might say that he made less than this because he had his crew to pay and ship repairs to make. This is true; 8) Triangle.

PHOTOGRAPHS, SAND © RICARDO DE MAURO/STOCK.XCHNG, CHEST © JANINE CHANCE/STOCK.XCHNG

HOT TOPICS Pirates

Lesson 1 Treasure chest

Resources and preparation
● Each child or group will need: photocopies of page 53 on white or brown card, scissors, glue, pencils and plasticine. This lesson can be adapted to form part of your Pirate Day.

What to do
● Ask the children where they keep their clothes and other belongings at home. Then ask where they keep them or carry them when they go on a journey such as on a holiday. Elicit the use of suitcases and other forms of luggage.
● Tell the children that sailors on ships stored all their belongings in chests. They had to be made of tough material and construction to stand up to being thrown around and piled up with other chests in a ship.
● Give out the copies of page 53 and tell the children that they are going to make a pirate's chest. Explain to the children that there are only two parts to cut out to make the chest and its lid.
● Draw the children's attention to the small illustration of a chest on the sheet and ask them to draw similar metal strips on the lid and surfaces of their chest. If it helps the children to visualise the chest, let them cut

out the parts of the chest and lid first. Make sure they take care when cutting around the tabs.
● Tell the class that pirates put their initials on their chests, and ask the children to put their initials on the two short ends and on the lid. If they have chosen a pirate name in Theme 5 Lesson 1 (see page 41), they might like to use those initials.
● When the children have finished drawing and writing, let them cut out the chest, if they haven't already done so, and fold the card so that the metal strips they have drawn are on the outside of the lid.
● Let the children glue the tabs to fix the sides of the chest together. Then ask them to do the same with the lid.
● Tell the children to bend the card along line A–B of the lid a few times then attach the lid to the chest.

Extension
Tell the children that the chest would be held shut by a big lock. Show them how to make a small plasticine lock to match the one shown in the picture. This can be pushed in place over the front part of the lid and the front of the main part of the chest to hold them together.

PHOTOGRAPH © PETER ROWE

Lesson 2 Pirate raids

AGES 7–9

Objectives
- To learn about the tactics of a pirate attack.
- To make a frightening Jolly Roger.
- To identify the weapons used in a pirate attack.

Subject references
History
- Find out about events and people by studying an appropriate range of sources including ICT-based sources. (NC: KS2 4a)
English
- Identify the use and effect of specialist vocabulary. (NC: KS2 En2 5a)
- Comment constructively on drama in which they have taken part. (NC: KS2 En1 4c)
Design and technology
- Generate ideas for a product after thinking about what it will be used for. (NC: KS2 1a)
- Measure, mark out, cut and shape a range of materials and combine components accurately. (NC: KS2 2d)

Resources and preparation
- You will need: a large green towel to make an island; large sheets of blue paper or fabric to put around the island; a sloop from Theme 1 Lesson 1 (page 9); a galleon from Theme 1 Lesson 2 (see page 10); a Union Jack without the red diagonals, a Jolly Roger and a plain red flag to fit the sloop; a large red flag; audio recording equipment (optional). Each child or group will need: page 54, materials to make Jolly Rogers (these could include black, red or white paper or cloth, glue, black and red felt-tipped pens). Visit www.kipar.org/piratical-resources/pirate-flags.html for ideas. This lesson can be adapted as part of your Pirate Day.

Starter
- Set up the towel as an island. Make sure it has some hills that the sloop can be hidden behind. Add the paper or fabric sea. Hide the sloop and place the galleon in front of the island.
- Tell the children they are going to learn some pirate raid tactics. Move the sloop out a little from behind the island and say that a pirate in the crow's nest sees with a spyglass that the galleon has fewer guns than the sloop and appears to have a smaller crew.
- Stick the Union Jack on the sloop and explain that pirates often falsely flew the flag of a friendly country to mislead their target.
- Tell the children that the pirates sailed their ship towards the galleon's stern or bow to avoid the cannons in its side. Ask the children about the course they should take to do this, and move the sloop accordingly. Now swap the Union Jack for the Jolly Roger and remind the children that this flag was used to frighten the crew of the galleon into surrendering.

What to do
- Issue page 54 and point out the flag symbols (also see page 41). Explain that the symbols were usually white but the heart and the skeleton could also be red. There could be red spots below the heart to represent dripping blood!
- Let the children design and make their own pirate flags. Suggest that they can use other images, such as an axe or a gun, if they wish.
- Tell the children that if a crew did not surrender, the pirates would change the Jolly Roger for a plain red flag (swap the

flags on the sloop). Explain that this means they will 'show no quarter'. If the children have done Theme 4 Lesson 2, ask them what it means. (Show no mercy.)

● Tell the children that the pirate ship would then come up to the galleon and the pirates would throw grappling irons (shown in the right of the picture on page 54) into the rigging to link the boats together.

● The pirates would then shout loudly to frighten the crew. If appropriate, you could get the children to shout, 'Give us your gold!' in a menacing way, and record it so they can hear what it sounds like.

● Tell the class that the pirates would then attack with a range of weapons. See which the children can identify in the picture. Tell them that a kris is a sword used by Chinese pirates and that a musketoon is a musket with a short barrel. Explain that pistols and muskets used gunpowder and sometimes the powder got wet so the guns would not fire. When this happened, pirates used their pistols as clubs (see the cabin boy in the picture).

Differentiation

● Less confident learners might need help identifying the weapons and perhaps in reading the labels.

● More confident learners could think of how they would have used all the weapons. Would they have used several at once or some then others? If the latter, elicit that they might have used guns and bow and arrow first then bladed weapons for hand-to-hand fighting.

Assessment

The children could be assessed on the quality of their flags and the way they worked out the identity of the weapons.

Plenary

Let the children display their flags and ask them to think of themselves as the crew that is being attacked by the pirates. Which flags would make the crew surrender?

Outcomes

● The children can understand the tactics used by pirates in an attack.
● They can make a scary Jolly Roger.
● They can identify weapons used by pirates.

Lesson 3 Slaves

AGES 9–11

Objectives
● To understand that slaves were considered valuable cargo.
● To use skills in comprehension and calculation to answer questions on information.
● To try and imagine a little of what it was like on a slave ship.

Subject references

English
● Scan texts for information.
(NC: KS2 En2 3a)
● Imagine and explore feelings and ideas, focusing on creative uses of language and how to interest the reader.
(NC: KS2 En3 9a)

Geography
● Use atlases.
(NC: KS2 2c)
● Find the locations of places.
(NC: KS2 3a)

Mathematics
● Make connections in maths and appreciate the need to use numerical skills and knowledge when solving a problem.
(NC: KS2 Ma3 1a)
● Use mental methods, use a calculator.
NC: KS2 Ma2 1a)

ILLUSTRATION © LASZLO VERES/BEEHIVE ILLUSTRATION

Resources and preparation
● Each child or group will need a copy of page 55, an atlas, a calculator, paper and pens.

What to do
● Tell the children that pirates sometimes raided slave ships. A great deal of money could be made from slaves, and when they attacked a slave ship they took the slaves and sold them. Some pirates became slavers – people who traded in slaves.
● Hand out copies of page 55, atlases and calculators. Tell the children that in this part of the lesson they will be looking at the slave trade as a 'business'. Emphasise that there was terrible suffering for the slaves and explain that they will look at one aspect of this later.
● Give time for the children to read through the information then attempt the questions. Then go through the answers as a class (see the notes on photocopiables on page 48).
● Tell the children that many slaves were

set to work on the sugar plantations in the West Indies. Slaves were also sent to the British colonies in North America to work on the tobacco and cotton plantations. In time these colonies became part of the United States. The use of slaves made many plantation owners very wealthy, but some people knew that slavery was wrong. Slavery became illegal in Britain in 1833 and in the USA in 1865.

Extension
● Ask the children to lie on a clean floor close together, side by side and imagine that they are slaves chained together on the deck of a slave ship. Say that the height of a table represents the deck above them and it too is full of slaves. Tell them to imagine that it is dark and dirty, with no ventilation, and that the deck is tipping from side to side as the ship sails the great distance from Africa to America.
● Ask the children to write what they imagine it was like to be a slave on a slave ship.

Theme 6 **Treasure chest**

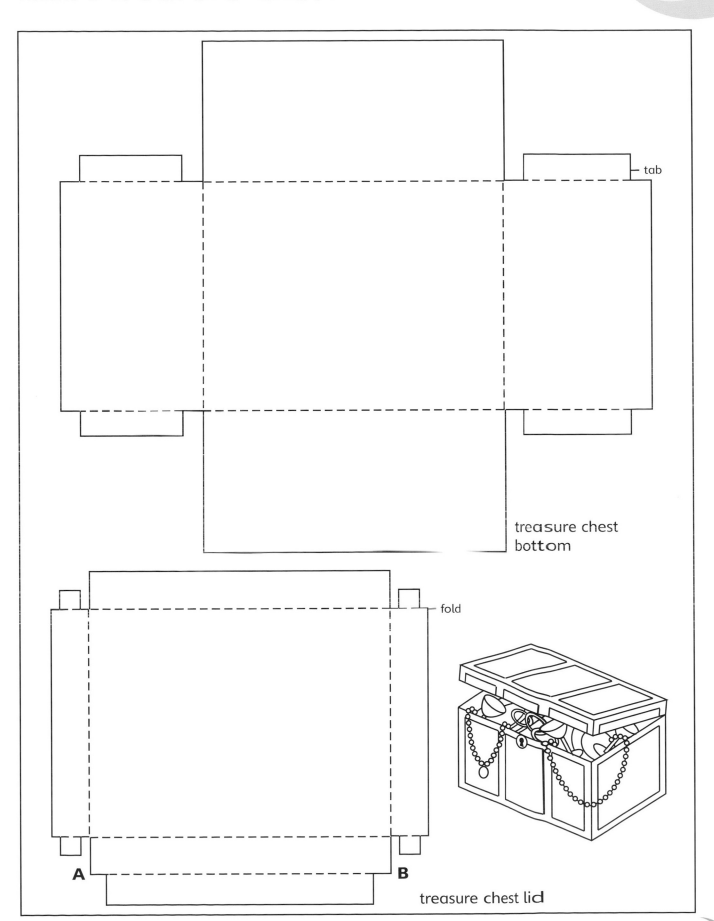

— tab

treasure chest
bottom

— fold

A   **B**

treasure chest lid

Famous pirates

BACKGROUND

When asked to name a pirate, children and adults will often not distinguish between real and fictional ones. Blackbeard, Captain Kidd, Black Bart, Henry Morgan and Anne Bonney were real pirates and it is their life stories that have inspired authors to invent fictional pirates such as Long John Silver and Captain Hook.

The story of Captain Kidd on page 78 is much simplified. In his early life he seems to have been a successful privateer and merchant. He married into a wealthy family and became well respected in New York. He had two children and enjoyed family life. However, in middle age, he set out on an adventure as a privateer. This went disastrously wrong, through bad luck and bad judgement, and resulted in him turning to piracy.

THE CONTENTS

Lesson 1 (Ages 5–7)
A pirate song

The children learn some of the commands of a bosun's whistle, and a pirate song. They can perform actions with the song.

Lesson 2 (Ages 7–9)
Pirate stories

The children draw on their work on pirates and the life of Captain Kidd to create their own pirate.

Lesson 3 (Ages 9–11)
Choosing a captain

The children debate which of four candidates should be the captain of their pirate ship.

Notes on photocopiables
Off across the Oggin (page 77)

This piece requires two competent descant recorder players. The music isn't technically demanding but there are no rests and it has quite a bit of momentum, so it will need thorough practice before being played up to speed. Only one recorder should accompany the verses as it will then be easier to hear the voices, but a second (or possibly more) recorder should join the chorus for extra 'oomph'.

There are quite a lot of words to fit to this tune, so the piece should be practised slowly. It might be worth talking through the words first, using the rhythm of the music. When the children are ready to sing the melody this should be done slowly so that they can see how the words fit together with the music.

Captain Kidd (page 78)

This story of Captain Kidd and accompanying questions can be used as a trigger for the children to make up their own pirate stories. Answers: 1) William; 2) Scotland; 3) A privateer; 4) A pirate; 5) 50; 6) They used oars to row it; 7) No. His ship was hit in his first raid and he was chased. The next two ships he raided were only carrying cheap cargo; 8) He would have been a free man; 9) He gave away money to his friend; 10) 54.

Page 79 Who should be captain? (page 79)

The sheet provides details of four pirates, which the children use in a debate to decide which one should be their captain.

PHOTOGRAPH © PETER ROWE, MODEL © EARLY LEARNING CENTRE

Lesson 1 A pirate song

Resources and preparation

- Each child or group will need page 77. If performing the song on Pirate Day the children should be in costume. You will need a whistle or recorder and a bell. You could ask a musical colleague to play the music and record it for use in class.

What to do

- Blow a whistle. Ask the children what it is used for. (Drawing attention.) Explain that when a ship was in a storm it was difficult for the sailors to communicate as their voices could not be heard. Therefore, the bosun had a whistle, which he used to send orders. Demonstrate some examples and encourage the children to learn the whistles and respond to them:
Blow one high note: stand still.
A high note that changes to a low note: carry on.
A series of short high notes: the bosun's mates should come to him.
A low note that changes to a high note: haul a rope or hoist a sail.
- Tell the children that sailors made up songs to help them do their work on ships. The songs are called shanties and some of them have pirates' names in them. Recall the pirate names learned so far.
- Tell the children that they are going

to learn a shanty that has been specially written for them.
- Help the children learn and perform the song on page 77.

Extension

- The song could introduce or end Pirate Day. Tell the children about a ship's watches (see page 34). The beginning of the performance could be marked by the ringing of the bell twice then a pause then twice more. The recorder could then be played as a bosun's whistle and the children could sing the song. They could put their hands to their ears in line two ('list'), mime pulling on ropes when singing 'Heave ho'. Each time 'Calico Jack and Anne Bonney' is sung different boys and girls can jump out of the chorus and swagger about.
- You could make a sail to drop when 'Set the sails' is sung and have a pirate flag to hoist. The children could mime climbing the rigging, using a spyglass and point South, East and North-west. They could jump about and raise their fists and pull faces in the last line of verse 3. They could waggle their fingers and smile on the word pleasure. At the very end, blow a whistle twice to bring them to attention and ring the bell twice, pause, twice, pause, twice, pause, twice to mark the end of the watch.

AGES 5–7

Objectives
- To learn about the bosun's whistle.
- To learn a song.
- To perform actions with the song.

Subject references
Music
- Use their voices expressively by singing songs.
(NC: KS1 1)
- A musical activity that integrates performing and appraising live music from a different time.
(NC: KS1 5a)
Physical education
- Create and perform dances using simple movement patterns.
(NC: KS1 6c)

ILLUSTRATION © LASZLO VERES/BEEHIVE ILLUSTRATION